TIME PIECES

◆

RELLA LOSSY

TIME PIECES

---

a collection of poetry

1944-1996

BY

RELLA LOSSY

◆

with drawings by

SUE SOMMERS

JUNE FELTER

JOAN COBITZ

RDR BOOKS • OAKLAND, CALIFORNIA
A ZENOBIA PRESS BOOK

My thanks to the editors of the following publications in which
some of these poems first appeared: *Critical Quarterly, The
Western Review, Prairie Schooner, ETC., Chicago Review,
Kingfisher,* and *Prism International.*

My thanks to those who encouraged this project: particularly, my
immediate family, Frank, Panna and David; three artist friends;
astute readers, Richard Silberg, Will Baker and Jim Schevill; mem-
bers of my cancer support group; Michael Lerner and the
Commonweal staff; Diana Cohen; Natalie Roberts; Jean Fargo;
and Wale Engelmann.

Library of Congress Cataloging-in-Publication Card No. 96-092079

Lossy, Rella, 1934-1996
Time Pieces/Rella Lossy
p. cm.
ISBN 1-57143-060-1

Manufactured in the United States

RDR Books • P.O. Box 5212 • Berkeley, CA 94705

Contents

II. THE MIDDLE AGES – *page 47 –*
with drawings by June Felter

III. EARLY ON – *page* 97 –
with drawings by Joan Cobitz

For Frank

*Whose profound love has sustained me
through sickness and health
and without whom this book
would never have been written.*

I

METRONOMES

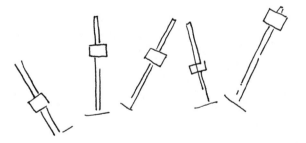

Drawings by Sue Sommers

Termites

"I see a door, I open it."
So says the termite man
inspecting the armpits
of my house.
"Some areas, I will have to write
'No information,'
Couldn't get in deep enough;
Too much stuff in the way."
(veils of Scheherazade)

"You want I should drill holes
in the stucco?"
My stomach quakes.
Can't a woman's house
be other than her body?
These sweet men
methodically going at us
to nail, prime, mend, redo, paint,
drilling holes in our spines,
plumbing deeply as they can,
wanting, always needing more information.

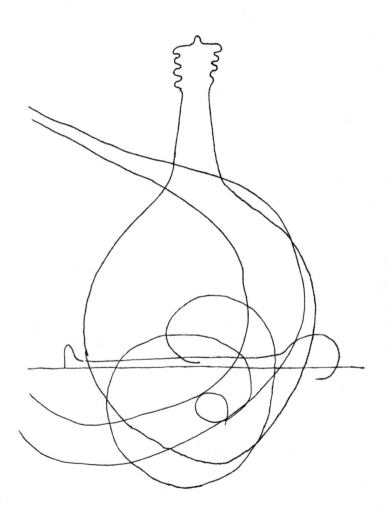

Tunnels

The light bulb by my bed
went out this morning
no warning sounds
no flickering
just a sudden
departure

Like approaching
a black tunnel at dusk

My friend
hates entering them
meets her fears in their hushed centers
where the walls are damp–darkest
and when traffic stops in the tunnel
she locks all her doors
takes off her rings
and weeps
straining to catch some light
from oddly spaced bulbs
growing dim on the narrowing walls

As I've used my bed light
the one that's gone out
to quench
the tight stomach
flickering heart
the long wail of traffic
trapped in the tunnel
as far as the mind can see

Me & My Tumors

There they were: I could see them.
Lying on my back during the body scan,
being obediently still,
but with my head turned slightly
I saw on the monitor
small perfect dots on my ribs.
How do you do? I asked politely.

— What?!

They speak as one, or did that day.
Now they have found their own songs.

How do you do? Who are you?
What are you doing here?

They twinkled and stirred their wings.
— We're making mischief!

One especially rambunctious little tumor
        pinched me hard.

Ouch! I said.
And like a stubborn Peter Pan,
        he crowed delightedly.

Oh, I said, you're pleased.
— Quite! cooed the fledgling.
And the other echoed, Quite! Quite!

Little round button birds, fly away.
— Can't, said a wee one.
— We're stuck.

Stuck?

— Yep! Stuck. Like tar.

— You Silly! said another. We don't use tar,
and she ruffled her feathers.

— We use Super Glue!

Oh, I said, that is most solemn.
— You bet! they said in chorus.

Sometimes they sing a motet,
sometimes a round,
a few excel at arias,
others cantatas;
they know many impish songs.

Go, little birds, leave this tree.

— Should we?

You could, I say.

— We don't know; we like it here.

Do you, now.

— We do!

I like it here, too.
— Then we'll be together!

For now, I said. But then . . .

— Then what?

Then you must fly off, move on.

—We're yours.

No, not really.

And so we argue
in song or hard pinch;
we try to work it out.

Go, little birds. You must.

— So you've said.

Yes.

And a little shy one looked up at me:

— I'll go.

Will you?

— I'll try.

Good, I said. Try. Fly away.

And she did. She tried.

Signals

One night, the wind got fed up.
Then the doorbell rang.
At three in the morning
I didn't know the wind had its limits.
"Don't answer it," I said.

It rang again.
And again.
And again.

Going to Arcadia with my Daughter

I could not let go of her,
so pleased that she had really come,
after the conspiracy to keep her out:
"There are no more tickets!"
they had shouted at the box office,
"Don't even bother coming down!"

I know better:
we *always* get in,
nothing is *ever* sold out,
even a small theater like tonight's,
so I stalk a woman by the door,
whisper, "You're selling, right?"
and buy a ticket from her.

Then the daughter doesn't show;
the time before curtain
grows shorter;
I leave the precious ticket
with her father,
go in, take my seat,
and grouse;
she's thrown away the treasure
I have found for her;
my mouth tastes bitter.

Then her father comes in
and, with a casual smile,
says she's made it:
she had stopped by the theater,
he'd handed her the ticket through the car window,
she'd gone and parked, and she's in the lobby now.

And once again I am the smug, jungle warrior woman,
savannah predator, bringing down game for my young one;
Mother Provider, even on crutches, even bent over, misshapen;
I am gaudy with triumph;
and so at intermission
when she crosses two aisles to meet me,
I will not let go of her, hold her tightly around the waist,
tell the pre–theater, near–miss story over and over,
not caring about *Arcadia* any more.

She has come, she has parked,
she has entered the lobby before the curtain rose.
We have won against nay–sayers, pleasure–deprivers.
We, the spontaneous fire–makers, have battled
and ignited the spirit again.
I do not want to release her.

Only the stern dimming of the lights
makes me finally let her go.

Not Too Close

When others had it (Nancy, Helaine),
I wanted to look away,
not hear, not see —
I wanted no part of their pain,
their misery,
I said to myself: "Not too close,
Don't get too close.
They say it's not contagious,
but they lie."

Now I've got it.
got it bad,
and still I want to get away,
not hear
these cancerous whispers
shuffling through my bones.

I ache, I ache
for home.

The Coach

The written instructions:
"Keep the coach
between arrows."
Curtained coaches,
French ones, Italian,
plumed coaches rocking,
wheels straining in mud,
horses snorting and rearing,
bows loosing fine–crafted arrows,
hissing through the sky
like peregrine falcons.

But my coach is none of these;
mine is a gauge on a breathing device
to stretch out the lungs,
an "inspirometer"
to loosen the grip of
expiration;
the clear plastic coach
rolls between numbers
in rocking milliliters:
500, 1000, 1500 —
I strain against them,
alert, earnest, loyal,
trying to keep my coach
between arrows
while I inspire
and breathe
and breathe and
inspire.

_Slope

She had come down the slope too far
to climb back up.
How did I get in this position, she asked herself,
not remembering what impulse lured her,
what destination she had imagined.

Now she was stuck,
her fingers digging in short scrub
giving way on the slope,
her feet jammed deep into the dirt.

She was thinking and
not thinking,
her body wanting to
hurry and follow gravity,
hurl her down,
be done with it;
her mind saying,
WaitWait!
think this through:
if you edge your arms this way first,
then that,
carefully adjust your legs,
you can gradually, safely,
make your way down
without panic.

Between panic and denial,
is that the slope?
I am on it again.

sliding down prickly dirt,
desperate fingers grasping,
this time not wanting
to reach bottom;
both mind and body saying,
WaitWait!
stay where you are.

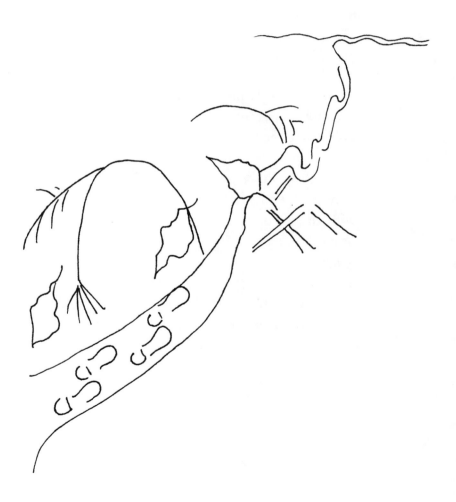

Camille

I imagine I am Camille:
my torso twisting
like a limp stalk of celery,
bones crumbling
like second–day bread.

Or tumors erupting
from the skin,
Like witches' wens,
like toad warts.

None of these do me any good.
I cannot project my death
as if I were the lead actress.

More likely, I'll be given
a smeared, unreadable script,
without directions
or blocking.
Stage center,
abandoned by director and cast,
the working lights out,
alone on a vinyl stool,
puttering with my props.

Shadows

I use this page
to measure the distance between us,
try to get closer and closer,
eager, ready this noon;
still I shield my eyes
from so much brightness;
suddenly, a cloud
drops over me
and the heat is gone.

And now it's back.

I cannot bear such brightness;
my script creates shadows
to keep us apart,
reminding me that I can never change
for more than an instant
what lies between us:
eternal dark.

Returning Calls

I will not return their calls.

Traveling through radiation,
through chemo,
I roam in a country
whose language does not translate
across boundaries;
my itinerary, freakish;
my emotions
open, strewn, scattered.

No one else can help me anyway,
with their damned success stories,
their you–can–do–it smiles.
I will not return their calls.
How do they know I can do it?
Do they think _I_ know I can?

I hate the miracle books
friends send —
wheat grass, coffee enemas,
guided imagery, God —
I want to burn shelves
of snake–oil promises,
won't meet
with a "victor," "survivor,"
whatever she calls herself,
the one wearing
hat, make–up and jewelry,
while I clutch my dirty bathrobe,

wondering how I can
live through the next fifteen seconds.

I will thrash against them all,
I will not reach for the phone.

_Interstices

I grieve for my life.
Not on a regular basis,
but between raindrops,
between doing and being,
between feeling connected,
feeling alone,
blue and green,
land and water.

During the word
difficult to pronounce,
I create a brass urn
for myself,
ornate shrine
amber candles,
grief the flame,
grief the breath
that blows it out.

Sentence

How harsh the uncertain night:
never knowing
if the moon, so full, so bright
will dance me light awake,
or if the hour will bark
like a guard:
"Your time is up."

_Metronomes

The heavy metronome base,
gleaming with walnut oil,
sits on a level surface
of absolute perfection.

You remove the cover,
and in that moment
the tempo is still yours:
you will not be rushed
nor slowed
nor shoved by the rising crowd.

You linger over the slider,
slowly, carefully, edging it down,
or up, to whatever pace,
any tempo your blood desires.

You hold back death
an immeasurable second,
holding, holding,
until finally
you let go.

And suddenly
the metronome flails
from side to side,
you are taken prisoner,
shackled by the meter.
Row upon row of metronomes,

ruthlessly click their tongues at you,
bind your hands, your feet,
your musical heartbeat,
casting you out
on the hard sounds of time.

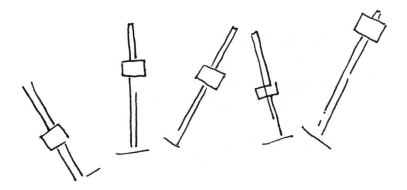

Ride

The young woman next to me
sleeps contentedly.
When she wakes, she asks,
— What kind of cancer do you have?
— Breast, I say.
— Mine's ovarian. I'm
on Taxol, she says,
That's why I have no hair.
And she giggles.

We leave together,
Get in the elevator.
— Someone picking you up? I ask.
— My Dad. You have a ride?

I want to say,
What a ride we both have:
You in your twenties,
Barren, unwed;
Me in my weathered sixties,
Riding our carousel horses
Reins crumbling in our hands,
Riding blind, feeling gagged,
Without hair, without breasts,
Grabbing at hope's brass rings,
Holding on for our lives,
Round and round we ride,
Dizzy from going up, going down,
Rising and falling in time
to tinny calliope music

that comes from behind
the thick, painted screen.

— Yes, I have a ride.
— Well, then, she says,
her smile like pink cotton candy,
See you later!
— Sure, I say. Later.

Comfort the Body

You say Comfort your body.
It barely serves me anymore,
a graceless encumberance,
in a dancing world.

But comfort it I have,
bathed it in warm scented waters,
dressed it in soft fabrics.
I have tried to stare
into the pool of my life,
a loving Narcissus.

This body, however, resists,
holds firm its threat
to plunge me once again
into stinging waters of pain;
I plumb for soundness
in a rocky harbor
of body and mind,
maneuver as best I can
for safe and steady space.

Writ on Water

I write on water
arms dripping on the page
trying not to sink these lines
in the bath
where I find I must go
my soul attended
by the tiger kitten

I retreat to this white tub
to float away
on a warm wet belly

while the furnace fan
gilds the air
with hypnotic chant
and the cat
purrs me through sea foam
she having fallen in twice
while I fall in daily
needing to steady
the tides
of my watery spine

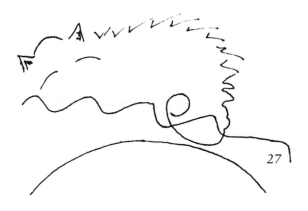

The Ocean

I wanted to see the ocean
and began my journey
in a wide arc
reaching towards pine trees
sloping dark ahead,
the path of bark and stick
pushing me closer
to a grove of seeming death:
pine limbs twisted, fallen, snapped,
dents, pitfalls everywhere
in the soft loam.

I lunged in,
thinking there is no ocean
at the end of this road,
but so awed
by tall black trunks,
dead leaves, withered cones,
that I could not stop
one trembling foot
from following the other.

Stumbling deeper,
I wanted to call for help,
retrace my steps.
Moss clung to my coat, my hair.
Suddenly, there I was,
balancing against the steep edge of the cliff
within a level space just large enough
for me to watch the ocean break
upon the ragged shore below.

Rocks

These rocks are written upon,
even those from a factory
that line this path
hugging the poison oak,
even that which we call gravel
so that no individual stone
can have a special name of its own,
even those pebbles have writing on them,
creased, lined messages in code,
tumbled carelessly against cracked earth.
Something has been written on these rocks.
We may try to read,
or toss them off the cliff
into the sands and washing sea below.

Cold Dark Glass

The water drips on cold dark glass
first quietly,
then like shot,
turning amber,
rippling with the wind,
but even now as we speak,
it drums much faster
so none runs smoothly,
it has changed in just this instant.

Suddenly, the rain is gone,
the tears are gone.
We have dried them
with cloths of medication, protocols,
pain control, menu meetings, celery sticks —
(they have been there two weeks already —
when should we throw them out?)

All the vague weeping
is dulled once again
by the clanging of doors;
we change from quiet to noise,
from dry clouds to rain
that floods and ruins
our carefully carpeted floors.

Sunday Morning Visions

Last night
I dreamt of poor Piglet,
tranquil Ohlone Indians,
and a one–armed lesbian guard.
Why *do* these visions
forage within
the hollows of my mind?
Answers growl from branch
to branch,
or bounce like lemons
on freeways.
Blessèd are they
whose eyes open or closed,
control their visions.
I am not one of those
this grey–skied Sunday,
for today I know
the dying trees outside my window
will prey on me,
unless I summon
a disordered splendor
of dream.

Inside and Out

Inside, the sofa beckons,
the warm rug teases your toes,
silence clings to the walls.
Outside, the wind
shouts in your heart,
sand blows in your ear,
poison oak laps at your legs.

But if I go out, wet hair and all,
I might meet a fox,
a talking rock,
a shy tree.

Some risks are worth taking,
some only worth writing about.

Foxes on the Road

The first one was only
the shadow of a fox,
a furry rustle near trees.

The second fox looked at us an instant,
then continued his journey
through thick brush.

The third held us
fixed in his gaze,
then vanished.

The fourth fox dined openly on the road
near the doorway of Pacific House.
We crouched by the windows
and argued over what his entree was.

And if tomorrow I see a fifth,
will he walk tall on two legs,
carry a bell, a carved altar,
a basket of fire?

Silence

We walk in meditative silence.
With each step,
I hear seeds.

A plane climbs the clouds.
On every side of me,
saplings, growing.

The sky sends a long blue kiss
to earth.
Everything I see
Flies a little farther than before.

Leavings

for Wale Engelmann

How easily the leaves
give up the tree;
they do not hold on,
but yield with grace
to a season of whispers,
short suns, cold nights.

Or is it that the tree
gives up its leaves,
allows them to find
another mission,
but not easily;
the tree hangs on
to color in its life:
yellow birds
or orange or blue.

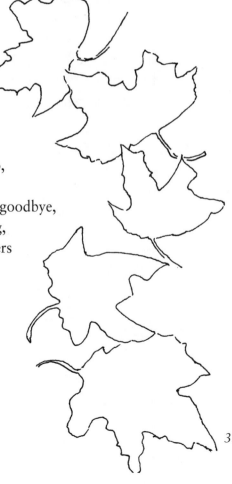

The tree holds on,
as stubborn ones will do,
will not allow leaves
to wave a simple, sweet goodbye,
fights against their going,
until the season's whispers
become a roar
of restless nights,
of grey moons.

Going

The whole world is empty
if you're gone,
my mother said.
Was it true?
Would a pit pursue us
in a maternal hungry quest,
shrivel our skins,
scoop out our eyes,
wrinkle our bellies?
As if my going,
even for a while,
would so endanger us,
we would be whirled out,
rolled on the edge of aching hearts,
broken like ancient coins,
never to be whole again.

Bird Swept

How quickly I've become
another.
Like a bird
that is swept left
when it meant to fly right.

I have gone into
a new shape
another size,
my body moving in
directions I cannot control.

The winds of cancer
not capricorn
pull my spine this way and that,
capricious winds
indifferent to my intent.

They pick me up
and joust me light
within this wary form,
and I, who not so long ago could run and leap,
I lumber wingless
towards a steep new sky.

Finally

If you think I'm finally dying,
what kind of new feathers will quiver in you?
Perhaps simple ones, like beginnings, middles, ends.
Or a desire to come visit me,
say hello, how are you, and goodbye.

Or you might find a window rock,
pristine vision through a stone
wherein each of you sees your own
immediate link to life, to lack of sight.

To believe I am _finally_ dying,
it is finally happening,
might be of some relief to you, too.

All that spirit time spent wing–wrapped
in the wax points on Daedulus,
in the downy shudder of Leda and the swan,
in the vicious fight of Oedipus and Laius.

We do not like to live without _when._
It forms our preludes, frames our posture,
forges pathos:
When to breathe, to sigh, to really live,
to finally die.

Insomnia

My sisters, too, are awake.
We curse, plead,
bargain with the clock
until we creep from bed,
drink warm milk in the kitchen,
linger in a scented bath,
swallow any pill we find,
slide ourselves into a book,

write a letter,
paint a few strokes,
pet the cat,
her purr
reverberating
through the bottoms of our feet,
burning with desire
to walk the moon —
each of us
a Lady Macbeth.

She was asleep, it's true,
when she waxed upright,
but she knew
what the rest of us know:
even if ever watchful and alert,
there is no escaping
night.

For Judy Hart
January 11, 1996

> (I have pains in my heart —
> a new symptom?)

Can you talk, I ask.
"Effort," you say,
and your eyes slide closed,
then you open them again,
"but I can listen,"
and you smile.
Are you in pain, I ask.
"No," you say.
Need anything?
"Cool water."

> (The pain is sharp,
> a blow to the left side,
> worse when I take
> a deep breath.)

I read to you.
Curled up like a kitten
on clean linen,
stroked by the sun,
you listen as if asleep,
but at the end of the poem,
you sound a faint echo
of your hilarious, hearty
explosion of approval.

> (It hurts, this heart of mine.)

You fall asleep now, truly,
and I sit watching you,

petting your shoulder,
silently saying goodbye.

I feel your breath on my face.
It comes cool and long,
reaches much farther
into the room
than it should,
just as your letters
reached far beyond your hands.

        (Is heartbreak a symptom,
        the body's pun?)

Before I came, I phoned
to ask what I could bring.
"Broken biscotti and a toilet seat,"
John said.
"Put that in a poem."
Now he races through the house,
trying to stay ahead of death.

        Goodbye, sweetie, I say,
        I love you.
        You summon up
        a dreamy smile,
        answer in a whisper,
        "I love you, too."

        (My heart aches when I move;
        I feel the need to sleep.)

Judy Hart died peacefully at home on January 14, 1996.

Prayer to my Daughter

Now I lay me down to sleep,
I pray the Lord my soul to keep,
And if I die before I wake,
I pray the Lord my soul to take.

And *if I die before I wake...*

Lay my spirit in a lustrous bowl
and make a pilgrimage
to places we have shared:

The Lost Coast Trail —
Go to our first campsite there,
near calla lilies
some defiant housewife
sowed a century ago
(and bless her stubborness, too).

And the Yosemite High Country —
Where I landed my first bear bag
over a long branch.
We slept by a boulder–studded river,
dived in with raucous shouts,
the sun applauding us.

And then that stonescape
above the tree line,
where my shins bled
as we hiked a razor–rock trail,
the barrenness outside our tent
pocked as the moon.

And if I die before I wake . . .

Take my spirit to those places,
whisper me back into that earth,
that river, those rocks.

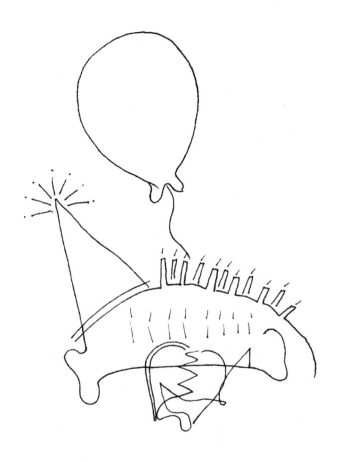

Birthday Dinner

No matter how old they get,
how many birthdays they've had
with ice cream and cake,
balloons, paper hats,
or, like tonight,
roast duck and wine,
with a poem of yearning
recited from memory
by the doctor daughter,
and the story of a bear
prowling the campground
from the drummer son

No matter how old,
there is still in me
the mother bone twanging:
have I protected them enough
from cold, from heat?
Is there more I should have told them
of love's knots and twists,
of the scavenging claw?

I want, I want
someone to tell me,
tell me I have given them all that they need,
they will never get cancer,
they will live eased forever,
their lovers revere them.
Tell me, for the party is ending
as night crashes in.

II

THE MIDDLE AGES

Drawings by June Felter

Accouchement

I'd like to wear a lamé gown
And an emerald cape with a hood,
And lie on black silk sheets in a bed
Carved of sandalwood.

Two nurses should carry the candlesticks
And three the samovar,
And the doctor could play castanets
Or strum the Spanish guitar.

Your daddy would sing as you burst out
And dance you into your bed.
Fur from the throats of bears and wolves
Would coddle your ruddy head.

Giants would paint you a story book
That witches and elves would write,
While twenty–six thrushes and thirty–four doves
Carol your first good night.

These are the things I want for you —
Nothing that's sterile, muted or mild,
but lightning, omens, and tempests wild,
a birth eccentric, like a planet, my child.

Apples in August

Eve was right:
pick the apple.
The tree, not the serpent, tells,
whispers a summer dream:
creation in the center of sweetness.

My hand wants it,
gropes the roundness,
strokes its blessing,
denies that angels might hiss
at my theft.

I prowl through the apple tree,
my foot in the fork,
setting my balance
to guard against breaking
of branches, trust, heart.

Ignore darkened fruit,
cracked, bird–pecked, scrawny nubbins.

Steal only the best,
the ripest, the sweetest
Idea of Apple.

A thief of autumn perfection,
I plunder the garden
of yearning.

White Morning

My child wakes
her muddy throat cracks dry air
the white morning screams,
falls in the ocean
my breasts, aching for rain,
break into thunder
her red lips suck white honey
we rock to the rhythm of apples and Eve
mother and child erupt from each other
from long ago
when fish filled the air
and man with a slippery cry
wrestled the mother

Before Dinner

Gingerbread Doors,
Sugared Sills,

Roof of Butter,
Floor of Honey,

My House a Warm Apple Pie,
Sweet Mama Dream,

Skitter–Scattering,
My Brood and I

Go Chattering, Clattering
All the Day Bye–Bye,

Trying Not to Eat Each Other Up.

Child, Your Eyes

Child, your eyes astonish me
More now than on your first born night.
Like a tooth rooted in urgency
You bolt into my sight.
Your head bangs like a door,
Knocks at my breast,
Then you're back to the dig, uncovering shores
Of secret rivers, boundaries that will not rest.
Who told you to bury your feet in the sand?
Ancestral whispers leave a nameless mark,
My arms open to their command
And you come running to embrace the dark.
I mother you with the blind past that mothered me;
We wade in ancient waters that we cannot see.

Mama with Little Children

Some day they will come at me
With cordial, mannered smiles,
But now these barnacles,
howling marauders,
Scrape me clean,
Peel off my masks,
Scale my dense walls.

Wanted like a criminal,
I turn myself in to them;
their need
puts meat on my bones.

_Gifts

These are the gifts from my son
On an ordinary Sunday
When the sun is full,
Warms us past the chill
Of separate streams:

   two black seeds
   live as lobster eyes
   twinned on a vine,
   held by trumpet bell
   blasted into ripeness;

   a leaf eaten by frost,
   or insect,
   or the circular flow
   of a leaf
   easing into yellow death,
   curling with grace;

   and one camellia,
   petals burning,
   its soft pink
   falling from symmetry,
   needing a center to stand.

These three brought without thought
Of what they mean or where they'll go:
Casual giving of love's hand.

In Small Portions

In small portions
daily
I could go
crazy
just a little
here a little
there a little
just a little
at a time

the black point
the white point
the red point
of sense
writes on my brain
small twisted ugly
letters
here a stare
there a stare
here a blank look
everywhere

but you should see me
smile!
I do!
and answer
yes yes yes

all the way home
while the piggy inside says
NO
and sounds like a bank
breaking

here a mouth
there an ear
it was once
full noon already
and I'd had myself
a nightmare
while preparing lunch
for you

but dear don't worry
I'm not really
in a hungry hurry
to go crazy
never
if at all
just bring a truffle
here
I'm there
everywhere
an oink oink

Higgledy

I carry a self
who goes higgledy–piggledy
all the live–long day.
She, I think, is for your
amusement.
(Whisper wills, iris arrested, rampaging rose)

Where did she come from?
Such a dippy flower.

Birthday

I'm about to be 42
and what goes out these days
doesn't necessarily
crawl back in
and what crawls in
doesn't always stay anyway

a sense that I'm older
sticks like barbed wire
and up is likely to
(as cummings said)
go down

untried directions dawn everywhere
how to tramp down one
and gather some new self–sense
but not walk myself senseless

as far as late beginnings go
it's not bad
to wait a little longer

If We Can Fly

In thy mother's kitchen
high above them all
we fly
clouds sweet as bread
and the oven warm earth
rising up up
to meet us
spin our souls
in thy mother's kitchen
and if we fly at all
if we can fly
then praise
wings pans spoons
and kneading hands
praise them all
spirits
and whatever molds them
that they rise

Fossils for Sale

Herring–like fish. Teeming.
Billions of years old.
Bright brown on the pale limestone
of the Green River.
Now on display.
For sale.

Caressable,
their spines tickle the tips of my fingers.
Their eyes,
their eyes wander the shallows,
looking for lunch.

Fossils.
Netted by time.
The river bed a hard, stone cradle
of flattened mummies.
They live on,
negatives against the false positive
of the mind.

Clumped, aswim
on a wooden shelf,
they leap forever.

Fossils. Graceful, mysterious,
amid abundant seas of deadly time.

Imitations

The ant crawls over
an imitation of an ant
that flies away

a leaf falls on
a grasshopper
whose wings are leaves

wood on a branch
wriggles past itself

       when roots
       roll down the jungle
       like snakes
       when water
       prickles mountain floors
       like bird beaks
       when clouds
       cleave the sky
       like buffalo
       creatures that are almost
       twins must agree
       on who shall be called
       an imitation

caterpillars   dragon heads
and the fine fins of angel fish
bumps   horns   silk nets
of cherry leaves chewing or being chewed

dissembling of semblances

the bloody tooth hovers in the lily
rises through the caged mouth
and eats both the zoo director
and his look–alike, the assistant

in a natural world
of comely imitation
it is not considered
bad manners
to eat and run

Someone Called

Someone called this morning
before flight time

before claw careening
bare gleaming wing

and the beak honed
before bird or insect

carried us off
chafing, stinging the sky

Imago — Imago
perfect eye of power.

someone called today
said Don't Go Away

fear stench clinging
for we need each other

with a song's yes
which we sing seldom.

listening to that call
Don't Go Away — Stay

the mind dry scratched
stung clouds still listening.

we go away anyway
won't stay to hear
we go jet deaf
miles out of tune

candescent roar
the brute drone

carried without a
thorn's care

for those left calling
landlocked, lone.

Hospital

Long frozen waves of waiting
for dangerous news,
black wings at windows.
Does death sound?
Will it start knocking
coldly like a pipe
this rain–choked day?

Upstairs, some man
is cutting my husband's throat.
Are you there, sharpening teeth,
Mr. Death? Are you like water?
Can you be everywhere at once?
Do I have more than three questions
this dim day?

I see clearly
sharp edges on strangers
sitting near me, floating;
we are all floating
behind blank window faces
of waiting.
Let everything blur:
black birds beating outside,
the turns in corridors,
cluster of nurses,
the green–masked doctor.

But I fear death's
grey graininess:
he takes pictures,
a portrait artist, Mr. Death.

Better for me to stay alert,
waiting,
watching the silent lens
for news.

Taking a Watch

Off the north coast of Minorca,
I float like a dark bottle,
(This the refrain: Your watch!")
waves peak, roll,
clouds dip, recede,
the mast lit golden,
(This the refrain: "Stay well out!")
my heart flails
towards a brittle beach,
chopped from the gold
of the island,
the smaller island,
("This the refrain: "Catch the wind!")
life folds like a sail,
crumpled the canvas
and gone the magic,
lost, no markers,
not a rag anywhere,
(This the refrain: "Hold course!")
someone will find this note
off the north coast of Minorca,
no land of minotaur
nor snowman,
but sun filtered
through Spanish lace,
I float in a dark net
off the coast of Minorca
where my course is set,

("Hold her steady!")
mutely from point to point,
while I hear
witches of the sea
come sound me close
to dance within
wave's mystery.

Hours

(I wound the clock at sea.)

the hours spun tight as a wet knot
minutes grabbed like crab claws

(I wound the clock)
the bead of noon dropped like rain
"One" came — a cloud
"Two" — a following sea
"Three" tumbled like a sail

(winding, winding)
"Four" banged like a wave
against the hull
and "Five" —

but what mattered was
(I wound)
was time's sound
coiling heavily down:
anchor chains in fog.

The Most Famous Sonnet Of Them All

The sonnet is an arbitrary form
aroused by poets from within
to disguise their shapeless terror,
comfort crowded, thrashing feelings,
to encase and label
what is messy and embarrassing,
or to give some simple, shared concern
the dignity of song.
A pattern of nature in man,
it gratifies the never quite lost need
to keep the world short,
and see that it behaves,
to slap life's hands and bind its feet:
the sonnet is a useful form of self–deceit.

Honey-Sweetie-Dear:
An Ode to California

Your moods are so weird, honey–sweetie–dear:
        pink blossoms peak in January,
there is or isn't rain,
       and when you pucker your mouth,
pine cones swoon down the Sierras.

We're all crazy about you — crazy!
        We pinch your bottom till you whine
and your valleys get flooded;
        we pour concrete down your ears
to make solid canals for our desire.

Sweetie, there's not a riffle, rill,
        or stroke of your light we don't want.
We've always grabbed at you with what we've had:
        pick–axe, stick of dynamite, crucifix, cyclotron.
What a pack of lovers crawled on your belly!

Once, when we were young and balmy,
        we kept time to your sighing,
and stroked your long blond hair
        and kissed your liquid eyes —
no wild clawing and biting then.

Them days is gone, dearie.
        We don't want to scare you,
but just 'cause there seems to be
        a few acres of you left,

fat and sweet as patches of the golden grape,
      that don't mean there ain't
ravage and some fast rape ahead,
      Honey. Sweetie. Dear.

This poem was commissioned and set to music by Elinor Armer
as part of her California Song Cycle.

Cremation in Bali

It doesn't seem right,
Not the way we expected.

Someone says: *It's really starting.*

A tourist unwraps an expensive lens,
Eager to capture the sacred second
in 35 millimeter color.

What's happening now?

The guest of honor lies swaddled in white cotton,
weighted down with thirty new sarongs
still bearing their sticky labels.

Who was he?

Gamelan players scramble away
in a black pick–up truck.

Have we missed something?
Where's the family?

One Balinese man,
in T–shirt, shorts, tennis shoes,
crouches at the foot of a grave.

Is he family?
A Frenchman yells at a Canadian woman:
she's blocking his view;
she tells him to go to hell.

Crisp palm flowers
the women made this morning —
eaten suddenly by bright flames;
then the frame of the cart,
fire crunching towards the center.
But did a priest light the match?

We hear only the whoosh of gasoline.
A tourist on a mound across from us
covers her mouth with her hand,
her face contorted in horror.

What is she seeing?

Ah! The poor corpse,
what we can know of it,
skinny, bare legs
pointing towards heaven.

The flames keen louder.
Fire tenders poke long poles
at the corpse.

Drop, damn you, drop.
Get the damned legs
into the fire trough.
Down and out of sight.

They won't move.
They stay up,
beseeching, accusing.

Finally they crumble
into the heat,
burst into flame.

Was that it?
The ancient rite of purification?

Naked, exposed,
we breathe the dark and bitter smoke
that covers us with ash.

Today

I'm fierce today.
I'll snarl, jump,
I'll eat your damned smile
if it gets too close.
Watch out for my elbow —
it'll crack a nose.
Watch out for my knee —
it will smash an eyeball.
It's not the same me today.
The fire I'll spit
will so singe you
no black hairs will linger
on your sheets,
and whatever you say,
I'll chew it up so fast,
you'll wish you never had a tongue.

There's a cyclone
on the loose today
in my jungle.
Stand back,
rejoice.

Well Waters

Hollow her body
her mouth a black tunnel open
that night she sang
through well walls
cobbled bones
sloping like stone
stiff as time falling
she held herself down
inhaling the smell
of cool well water calling

at night because at noon
she wouldn't enter her courtyard
lean over well rim
climb in
while bleak chickens
pecked dirty corners
the black dog chewed on dreams
and her seven children
danced a ring around the well

she waited till night
slipped from her bed
out the kitchen back door
and over the edge
not a sound from the moon
a crystal goblet sky

of stars washed over her
in the wet cold hollow place
her own
and no one knew till morning
where she'd gone

For Gordon

We live in secret
dim, jagged, voiceless space,
deep, stretching back
without beginning or end:
rain stops, the sun glows, fruit blooms—
none of this matters at all
in airless, inner space.

Often faces say nothing,
display our own expectations,
protect others from anguish
the way fog covers a river.

Gordon, we thought we knew you;
we did not.
You seemed strong, cheerful,
tied to life.
Did you think we would disapprove?
Did you call us once in a dream
and did we turn away?

We might have come;
we could have brought you
our own foolishness —
it's not so special;
we could have said,
the shepherd is like his sheep —
let us fear wolves together.

The river banks are high,
the tule reeds thick and gentle,
one hour is like another,
the sky darkens, fog gathers;
finally, the mind, like the tide, recedes.
Though you did not ask,
part of us went with you.

_The Contractor's Wife

The contractor's wife,
mother of three,
hid herself under the pepper tree,
laid herself down
on the fertilized ground,
took poison and died;
while the little ones cried,
and the freeway sighed,
and the sweet jets swooned on the blue.
That was the way
the contractor's wife
spent the day.
And what about me?
And you?

Department of Motor Vehicles (DMV)

We have come to the edge of the Sacred,
We have come for High Ritual,
We have come for The Test.
In the kiva of the DMV,
there is even music
to keep the heart from turning cold:
ring of phones,
finger click on keys,
lightest chatter songs
of applicants, suppliants —
though I long for
drums, bells, holy chanters.

Cold in the snow,
we huddle by the back door
to wait for the *savios*.

> In white deerskin from head to foot,
> no flesh showing,
> narrow slits for eyes,
> they come out of the mountains,
> off stone–faced walls,
> off cliff–sides.
> They rise from the earth's throat
> to prance down rocky breasts of fields.
> We see them from miles away,
> white specks on the mountain,
> dancing, leaping, strafing the brush

with white leather whips
as they come
towards the silent, waiting pueblo:
eerie judges,
punishers sent by the gods.

My son gets a hundred points at the start,
and for everything he does wrong,
he loses points.
Slash, slash goes the whip.

We overhear another test:
Sorry, says the wise one;
You tell me now you understand,
but now it's too late. Sorry.

Error is noted on the holy clipboard;
the strike is swift, impersonal,
harsh, red marks chafe the soul.
For that one,
Now is too late.

But my son has passed!
Let's go, he whispers with a grin.
This is a quiet kiva.
No six–foot leaps in the air,
to let his body blaze with triumph,
dancing past failures away.

But I want to shout:
LOOK AT HIM! THIS ONE!
MY SON! HE HAS PASSED!

Gravely, they take his picture, his thumb print.
In four to six weeks, he'll receive
the hallowed card,
the potent driver's license itself,
proof that he may wander among us,
initiate, member of the tribe,

For he has met and conquered
judgments of the faceless ones.

Backpacking with my Grown Daughter

In the wilderness
we lug forty pound packs.
Granite speckled peaks
watch with secret eyes
while the river runs towards,
runs away from us,
and dust rises, falls
on the old trail.

We talk of this and that,
are swept back and forth
across the icy river
that pulls us
one way, then the other.

Until she says, Stop!
and I wait patiently
while she gleans a campsite
from the earth:
This is the spot.
Camp here, she says,
Not anywhere else, No.
She is leader now —
I lay my head
where she calls heart.

In the morning
we boil water on stone,
brew fancy tea.

Then naked by the river
stretch our bodies
in the sun and dive.

Mother and daughter
stripped of home;
On our backs
the weight of all we are,
have been and done,
life–and–death bearing,
as it was
in the beginning:
the two of us
the sun
and wilderness.

Bars

I found
a parakeet perched on a truck
outside my house.
A former prisoner,
she recognized the hand
and curled long, thin claws
around my finger;
I whispered her into my kitchen.

Full of alien needs,
threatening at first to die,
she kept me up at night,
tending, cooing, warming her.
Why was I doing this?
Had I made an agreement with her?

When she recovered,
I let her be without bars,
a soaring through the house,
a brightness in the air, secure.

Inside of me,
she found a playful friend
long silent in a rusty cage.
She pecked until we fluttered
out on a melodic sky.

Workshop

We work in the dark shop of dream,
grief's storeroom,
and the time is still, is still
to beating bone, soft flank,
the mouth that aches,
ashes that blow
grey time over liquid eyes —
and all is darkness in our workshop.

In the still time, we use
hammers, saws, sandpaper, putty,
filler, and paint–soaked rags
torn from underwear, pajamas,
pillow–cases, sheets,
the darkest clothing of sleep,
dangerous rags, combustible,
we don't know when —
when, in the darkness of our workshop,
time stands still,
and rags of darkest desire
flame and flame,
and flame again.

Friend

Your silence stalks my jungle;
You are ready to pounce,
And I tread lightly,
Fearing the smell of rent flesh,
Pierce of your claw.

I cannot be still,
My hyena voice babbling at my bones
To steady the dark, jellied heart.

Will you bite?
Leap on my back?
Will you seek me out at all?

Nights pass; finally you come,
But I have stopped being afraid.
Your blades thrust cold,
You hurl stale angers,
Accusations overgrown with scars.

We stand clear of each other
Unable to fight to be together again.
Grimly, we let nets fall between us,
Our tense hearts tied,
Our tongues coated in sullen scum.
We thrash through the raw silence;
Then we lie.

My Breakfast with Diana

We have sat on hard rough boards
drinking our coffee,
watching time run out
on meters, marriages,
watching people
on their way to work,
to grief,
a story here, a stinging problem there,
taste of bitter cinnamon and sugar,
tangy talk in sunshine
or in the cold dark morning air.

Subjects like gulls
wheel free
high in the sky,
and we rescue
bright scraps
to share with each other
from soaring, separate days,
a life brew
of wants and fears.

Often when we were younger
you said, Let's open a restaurant,
and so we did,
with doors unlocked,
with no address.

Poem for my 60th Birthday

When I was twenty, I said I love you
And began to climb.
On an empty stomach.
Without water.
Without proper shoes.
And without a map.
I was alone,
though someone else was there.

Looking down made me dizzy,
so I didn't.

The trail is tighter now.
My legs have grown so thin
they bleed when rocks graze the skin.

Before, I would smile my way up
Towards plateau,
mesa, or shimmering peak.

Before, I would smile my way out
of any pulling down,
Even grab and cherish some of the dirt
to sift through later.

Now I frown if I fall,
predicting precisely
the size of pain,

the healing time.
With care, now I look down,
distrust the trail,
Wear proper shoes,
Bear two water bottles,
I hardly see the sky at all.
Down has become the major direction.

Is that what we came for?
Is that what we want?

Not yet, not yet.

We must move quickly together.
Find whatever chase we can,
Bring antibiotics, bandaids,
Reverse gravity if we have to,
Buy the right clothes. Often.

And drink
the thrill of the upward reach
Drink whatever liqueur
still stalks us to climb on a dare.

Craft: For Bill

How do you do it? he once asked me
about this craft of mine,
words on paper.
If the drought ends,
and fruit trees triumph after rain,
and a bright geranium red
defies the heavy, grey–brooding sky,
it's not too hard.
But I never explained it really,
for poetry is an act
that matters only after it is done.

How do you do it? I wanted to ask him.
How do you live with a sense of time
so different from ours?
How do you hold on to bright blooms of hope
and still grapple with a heavy grey sense of doom,
not losing your joy
nor denying it to others,
not losing the desire to go on,
even in pain.

I never asked,
but I am grateful
to be witness to his craft,
his complex bravery
within the art of living and dying.

It mattered during all his time,
and matters still after it is done.

III

EARLY ON

Drawings by Joan Cobitz

Beached

The sun beams relentlessly
on the long beach of my life.
Everything shows:
gritty sand of small hurts,
knotty splinters,
dried moments of joy soft to the stroke of memory,
the damp strip of tide where the feet sink cool
against an ocean of uncertainty;
I am both hot and cold at once —
bittersweet imperfections in the light.

Bald Man Eats Banana

What if
we were created from fruits of the earth:
the jungle sounds a gong,
swamps become fountains,
birds carry nests in their beaks
and fly away screaming,
man runs bodiless through flame and water
falls on cabbage and has a head,
trips on persimmon and makes a heart,
grabs at broccoli and has a crotch,
sucks in honey and red pears,
finally assembles his parts,
and picks them all up with succulent fingers.

With barely a whisper,
paradise recedes into a business suit,
where a nice bald man
opens a brown paper bag,
takes out a banana,
and eats it.

Colors
    are qualities
and blue
    to you
       is not blue
in relation to
    what i see

      occasionally
LIKE NOW
    the rain runs through
       the redwood cones
and i can see
    the spray lunge
       at the panes
and then
    below
there is the blue
    i see
      a fabric
and an entity

WHAT'S GOING ON?
    the radio
and Mozart
    and birds in the unseen trees
      but also
five or maybe

six pale yellows
    set before this blue
transparent daffodils

and so
  their green stems
let the blue pass through
  and then
    you see
this blue
  is not the same
TO YOU
  as now
    TODAY

it is to me

Run

The urge
to get out
to run
escape
goes back
to the first
spinning sperm
rolling ovum
the womb door
the infant
unfolding
breaking out
of earth
into air
pushing words aside —
to leave Eden
the planet
palpate space
the will
running on
catching
fire

Contingency

Dismiss my apathy;
ignore my dismal face and fidgeting.
Say it's a mood,
that I need rest or love,
or polyphonic voices of a church.
I should have a good scrub and a powder,
blow kisses to the leavening night,
and spring will greet me when I wake.

Say all this, but be prepared
for a mocking shrug, a whining laugh,
the beast thrown in your face.
You and I are not contingent;
we have perfect intervals between us.
You and I can analyze, antithesize,
compare the magic of the dead scribes,
but we possess two mouths between our minds
and flesh between our souls.
So let us simply rub behinds
and pace our paved directions.

Danse Royale

She flexed in sleep, then tightened up her knees
And thighs for long, swift arabesques in air.
Her arms grew fluid as a black sea breeze
And left the arched wrists floating white and bare.
Each second met her turning smile or stare;
Each muscle felt the pulsing of the clock.
Her perfect time remained a hidden rock.

At dawn she eased her body off the bed,
Carrying her torso like a spinning top.
As high as neck could stretch she held her head
And when the teacher called, "It's time to stop,"
She watched the mirrored motion break and drop
And pledged that every future practice page
Would find her ready as an open stage.

An Eden angel whirling in a flame,
She scarcely heard the curtain when it fell.
She pressed the hands of those who came
Backstage and thanked them, even though she thought she smelled
Their ashen flesh and saw it puff and swell
On slackened frames of vagrant, shrinking bone.
Did those who praised her body disavow their own?

Ruth St. Dennis

She came before us
in a long black jersey gown,
laid a ream of paper on the lectern
and dared us look away.
Her words speared me,
I froze.
Her skinny wrinkled thumb
pinioned one page
after another,
letting each one go,
then hang there in the air,
suspended by her force of will,
until the moment
when she let it float down stunned,
the supple pages that she'd danced
still glowing at her feet,
so by the end
she was surrounded by her own determined
legendary snow.

False Alarm

*The multiple communication lines that were
supposed to provide backup if one or more of
them failed all ran together at one point and the
trouble occurred there. They no longer run
together at any point.*
        –Associated Press
        April 1, 1962

They no longer run together at any point.
So it's foolish to be frightened,
our defense has been enlightened,
and an accidental war
can't happen any more.
We've perfected the vast corps
of buzzing wires, clicking cables,
beeping radar, triple circuits,
everything syntonic, modern, electronic,
heavy signals flashing, "Notice and interpret,"
And they no longer run together at any point.

In the system of Great Powers
there are separate warning towers
that can activate jet flyers
any time the supple wires
send a message of attack.
We're quite ready to bomb back,
and we never have to guess;
they've fixed the awkward mess
in one junction, at one joint,

So that nothing runs together,
Nothing runs together,
Nothing Runs Together
any longer at any point.

The Hunt

I remember a harsh dawn,
a blizzard that had left the air
starched and dry,
fur, leather, wool, and heart
that were no protection,
the guns that had begun
with the first suffering light
in the sky, and the marching:
sullen, heavy, searching, separate,
each man trampling the brittle brush,
red–capped, neck straining,
some shouting, though the calls were cold;
and then the shots, puckering the air,
and later,
the earth soiled with gut,
dragged blood, a foot torn by a rock,
part of an ear,
the carcass being stretched between two pines,
the long knife shearing the skin.

I remember how we ourselves had practiced
firing at red circles on a nearby tree,
how we were bored waiting,
our bodies burdened and stiff,
how we missed our comforts,
wanted to go home,
and found talking to each other
dull and hollow,

how we brewed coffee
for the hunters
when they returned
and were glad to be of use;
but later, I grew afraid —
seeing each man squatting, restless,
eating and eager, gun ready,
finding they spoke little to each other
and hardly noticed us;
it was not fear of blood that I remember
but fear of my own patience
with their licensed lust.

Motel Prayer

Naked and perhaps benign,
my thighs enshrined in pink percale,
I am in a plastered, draped motel,
not far from a Marine guard.

A vinyl table by my bed
supports a Modern–Greco–Oriental lamp;
a puffed cherubic dome,
a frosted base that floats a studded shade,
a monarch's crown.

And in the corner, for a drowning,
waits a simple walnut bar,
formica case for ice and glass,
chrome shining like the Eastern Star;
two cast white plastic chairs
are nailed down like arms upon a cross.

A spirit sparks here,
a sudden altar on a Sunday night
in this my chapel and motel
with even soldiers at the door.

I kneel beside the aqua speckled wall
to plead: Whoever You May Be, deliver me
from all the world's lust and waste,
the outer symbols of an inner fall.
Make me austere
in this abundant transitory place,
and grant me grace.

My Father's House

My father's house is fraught with heavy carving
flowers dangling from the roof
a golden cage for a green bird

I walk in quiet Chinese slippers
take small steps
a fragile cloud a bubble

My father's house shakes with bird laughter
the feathered prince preens
silk fans shudder in the breeze

I wear peacock eyes
that see spring
even in the dead of winter

My father's house is a deep forest without doors
stretching through brambles
broken mountains dark muddied streams

and I walk with heavy boots
through gnarled brush
toes throbbing

My father's house never stands still
the body staggers towards it
and the mind trembles from the quake

Rough Red Patio after a Big Lunch

I am, in spite of the big dirty toe
     on that soft, stone–benched, napping girl,
     the jerking sputter of a grass cutter,
     pushed by tortoise shell glasses and man,
     the BmmmmmmmmmM, that unthinkable thing
     done again at exactly 2:07 p.m.
     by the pilot of jets (and deaths),
I am ruffling, drifting in the sun,
     fond and quiet, and in the air,
     (Put your legs down, Eve; they impart
     white tricot love.)
     rumbling, and broken by building tools,
I am shuffling with impressions,
     courting warm digestion's whisper.

Though the day promises time
     for roses and melons, hiding in forgotten places,
     being the animal I can never be and can't even remember,
     reading foot prints on pavement, thumb prints on doors,
My body bends for a caress.

Though the mind . . .
     (a remarkable ant, single, skitters on the rough
     red brick, going somewhere in the nuzzling sun)
Though the mind . . .
     (they talked of walking on water and the loss
     of faith. Wasn't it strange and oriental . . .)

Though the mind . . .

      (Why do people go around, walking down street or up;
      why does someone enter a room, or a marriage . . .)
Though the mind. . .

It insists on the jumbled, circuitous yawn.

Selves

Who is with me?
Selves, spoons, pencils, sparrows,
and Roethke, singing like a bird.

Who is within?
Dying cells, dumb heavy bars,
and the yawn of prisoners.

Whole selves, half selves,
and selves left over
from books and dreams
and angry veins unbled.

What a place — my head
feels like a big drunken bar
with no tender,
without a tender gesture in it.

Just shoving and lunging,
sneering and yelling,
before I fall on the floor
in mumbling rage.

Pick her up gently
with spoons or a pencil,
and she'll sing for her selves
like a sparrow.

Nonetheless

How smoothly my ballpoint rides
on this vermillion paper;
nonetheless, my back aches.

Department Store

Music guides us down aisles
where we glide through
racks of dresses and suits.

Suddenly, one of us leaps, spins,
the spine skids, the heart shies,
and she lies, eyes closed,
on the floor,
blocking the center aisle.

Policemen come,
murmur like spools.
Someone takes a coat off a Sale rack,
lays it over her,
and we study this grey Snow White,
anonymous, helplessly on display,
a reflection of ourselves
newly attired.

Men with a stretcher carry her away,
but the aisle will not be
emptied of her image.
We move slowly and sway
as the music brings back
our illusory sense of balance.

For Ivan

Young, you hunted in tide pools,
caught spiny shapes,
defined slippery faces at the water's edge.
You raced through silent Sunday alleys,
rattled garbage cans,
brought up half–filled bottles,
and rocked them back and forth
till they released their secret alchemies.

Paces ahead (you were always tall and fast),
you stalked neighborhood clocks
till you had cages full.
You sounded their alarms
or chose to stifle them.
You could unspring time's smallest wince,
then make it blink and howl again.

Grown, you peered in tide pools of the mind,
grappled with spiny demons hissing there,
supporting those whose feet slipped
towards dark waters' edge.

On Sundays, you pounced on flea markets,
rescued more wounded treasures,
still ached for alchemy.

Dark bottles, labels lost,
elusive demons,
needs clanging like alley lids,

you prowled and hunted.
Who is not caught? your father said,
caught like a clock,
the spring uncoiling
in our throats.

You chose to stifle the alarm,
a silent secret Sunday,
and now we're caged
inside the wince and howl
of time you cannot wind again.

Bird Vision

You see the bird?

No.

You don't see the bird?

No.

But he's there.
Above the trees.
The charred black branches
form a sky.

What trees?

The trees that stand
black, stuck,
their trunks swords
in the earth's side.

Where's the bird?

Above the trees,
flying.

Where are the trees?

I told you!
In the ground.

They're burned now,
but growing.
burned by winter's ice,
by winter's snow.

They're burned?

Then you see them?

O.K.

And you see the bird above them?

Sure, if you say so.

But I have nothing to do with it.
The bird is the whole idea.
You've got to be sure you see it.

I'm not sure.

It's not a symbol.
It's a real bird.
Aren't you even curious?

No.

Poetry Readings

Faithfully, I have put on my coat
        and gone to witness the man
who rose like smoke,
        opened his book, and began to read.
Not once could I close my eyes
        to let rivers flow by.

The people who came were
        like myself, some
reflections of a fun–house self
        with the deserted longings sticking out:
the flaunting girls
        trailing their long dark hair behind them,
the old ladies
        dry as fall flower beds,
the usual oddity, madman,
        most recently one without pants,
just a sheet furled between his thighs,
        who came in late, determinedly Hindu,
but painfully swaddled and loose
        in the noiseless room.

Noiseless, but at one reading
        I thought we would rise like fire
to consume the thin, cold, octogenarian bard;
        and at another, someone yelled,
"Emptiness! Shame!"

And I left with hecklers
who had the word.
It has never been right.
        I've gone hoping to find
God's burning bush upon the stage;
        instead, some man
read a poem off a page.

Lessons

Watch ironwood trees:
they grow two hundred feet slowly,
shed thin skin, grey skin, black skin
the moment they seed,
strip like wrinkled old men
in a Turkish bath.

Watch moths:
white, blue, chocolate,
red moths,
veined, pattern–faced moths,
fragile as an infant finger,
their floured wings hum softly
in the warm light.

Watch owls:
they squat on Monterey pines,
rattle the jays, glower at mice,
and big as boils,
haunt the pine's roots
deep down the earth.

Pray to
scathed trees,
cold moths,
moon–shackled owls.

Turtles

When completely unobserved,
Turtles become Princes —
When the moon bobs like a coin
tempting the greedy sea below,
and a crab in silent sparkle
brandishes claws sideways
on blue glass pebbles
slippery beyond count.

When unobserved, completely,
Turtles, in a quake of tortoise tumescence,
Crack their mottled protections.
The beach, crazed, sputters with shell.
Erect Turtles, male and female,
begin their naked, toothless pomp
up the gangling gangway
to the buckling boardwalk
where awaits them the
(who else?!)
King Crab —
to bless them gladly,
sharing his hopes at the end of an age;
Shining Turtle Princes
who welcome any future beach,
no matter how bleak and spiny,
who seek in every wave
a generous new faith
revealing order and meaning.

That's what my friend said,
and he added,
"There aren't any Real Laws
of Nature anymore
anyway."

Il David (Michelangelo)

I

David, wait a time,
and through night's deepest effort,
I can join you and the children,
skipping with the Florence sun and shadow,
laughing in the empty corners
of our proud, unfinished hearts,
staking short–cuts through the courtyards,
chasing past the red and green
mosaic Byzantine.
A shout, and like a hungry legion,
we take aim.
The foe's a sagging statue,
face and body in a garbled mass;
our passions, sticks and stones,
are freed on windless air.
The guard threatens a heavy hand,
but knowing that in two more bells,
the nuns will call us into class,
he lets us rush away.

II

David, bear a closer vision now.
I smell the fading tapestry,
the rotting colors in your gallery.

I shuffle down the shaded hall,
the littered walls,
and scratch past pagan, classical disguise:
the satyr moaning for a maiden's prize,
the hollow feel of bone and thigh,
the bronze duplicities,
until I find you, biblical,
and marble.   Marble:
molded mellow rose, foam smooth,
full muscle blown, warm pearl rubbed,
and ringing in the hard reflecting moon;
and in the final murmur of your form,
I touch a story and a song.

III

Perhaps you have come from a swim,
and the sling is a cloth,
and the tree stump a marker near the stream,
and you are smiling, refreshed,
thinking that no one ever lived before,
that all this world is a door
which only you can turn,
being young and open to the sun,
being young and not yet knowing
what you need,
and needing no one yet.

David, let me stay with you
where nothing happens but a day,
a branch that flowers on a hill,
and where —
David, be still,
The giant doesn't care,
and even if you win,
the children in the square
will not remember.
David, stay here.
This challenging,
this right to sweat and twist
becomes a hunger.
You are strong and clever;
do not be a stone
for fable's sling,
for as the world moves,
the mind revolves,
losing what the body gains.
David, remain.

IV

And so you do.
This is no vision now;
this is Italy
where you stand beautiful,
well–kept, admired by the tourists.

We are all of a kind, David.
We are loved and lovely
and we have our dreams
and our unguided time.
I turn and walk away
and hear the shallow echo of the floor,
and think tomorrow may be war
and we shall leave you here,
and someone else will find you
shattered: sling, a broken belt,
hand, a restless piece,
a relic of the jagged wrist,
feet split from hanging toes,
torso, head and pedestal,
a porous heap of limestone for a tomb.
Within that stone, I see you yet;
I feel the mark you made,
the splintering of my bone.

Once Upon A Time

for Kisa Lossy

Those days were like
no other days
in no other town
with no other people.
Sometimes there was nothing,
nothing worth doing,
nothing worth seeing.
There was only yourself,
talking to very fine people
of very fine things;
and more was important,
more was uneven,
than it has been since.
I mean, you can hear back
this long after
all of the detail,
for voices are clear
and faces are pressing,
walking in shade
under the trees,
and I mean, you learned
about love there.
And you learned.
It seemed
as if you could never stop learning.
There were so many ways
to look, to find,
there was so much yourself

to look at, to dream of,
there were so many people
to follow, to ask
so many questions,
and I mean
it was important,
being young there.

Aunt and Uncle

In his room, uncle dies into himself. His body is reaching, dragging all that's left of his social self off his face and under his skin. We say hello to him. He says hello skin.

In the dining room, aunt spoons sour cream over cooked pears. Through the thick, white juice, she sees back forty years, smiles over what was said.

In his room, uncle feels the insult of forty years ago. He twists inside his sheets.

In the dining room, aunt gives us a bear she made from real fur, a rooster studded with pearls, a blue felt octopus, creatures to win, to frighten a child.

In his room, uncle lies perfectly still, watching the war in his bloodstream. A large black roach sits stuck in his navel. His skinny hand plucks it off. The hole opens, widens. With greed, he pours himself in.

Ruins

The door is wide open
saying, Welcome, Welcome,
Come into my house, come in, come in.
I touch nothing yet,
I walk softly, I inspect;
I'm just looking, thank you,
in empty closets, open drawers, dusty corners.
My greasy lips kiss marble mantels,
brass door knobs, teak stair posts.
My eyes rattle, my pockets ache.
The ball and chain are swinging, smashing,
but I know how to work fast,
for I am the one who stole the gold boat
from the pharaoh's grave;
rubbed the queen's lace wedding dress
against his sweaty thigh, while burning the palace.
I am Marco Polo and Cortez and all their slippery whores,
falling in the river, drunk on each other's
greedy laughter;
I am also the one who tore her grey hair
and wailed into the ashes
when the soldiers entered the temple.
Now I risk myself simply,
leaning out a window,
twenty feet above quince and acacia,
banging at the sash with a sink pipe,
prying out stained glass
to hoard in my basement.

On the Edge

She thought:
I want to hug that elm tree.
She thought:
I'm on the edge;
If I do, I'll cry.

(A King Lear fool,
pulled by a string of feelings
banging against each other
like headstones.)

She thought:
If I touch that tree, I will scatter to the winds.
Am I just a pile of dry leaves?

The old elm,
its bark rough–ridged,
sends her rings of patience.
Which she cannot wear.
Her fingers swollen
with grief stones
with fear water.
(We will not bore you
with details.)

The tree's amputated arms
are a casualty of the war
between power lines
and what?

A war between
what we want
and what we want.

She thought,
I will go like a fool
to the tree
and hold it.

And later,
when there's time,
I will weep.

Goodbyes

I'll miss you.
And we know
I wouldn't say that
if I meant Don't Go.

Morning

Morning brings
brisk blowing
the wind howling
sweeping the world's floors
teasing trees
chiding simpering willows
all night it blew
cleaning between the teeth
the toes
of the clumsy
metropolitan giant
gulls huddling
under a freeway
boats moaning
at moorings
bridges bristling
steel bold
the wind brings
a hug and a squeeze
a cold sunny roll in the grass
take hold
all ways are clear
and plain to see
and all seems innocent

No Paint Nor Page

It is not the timeless before,
Nor the endless cries of knowable torture,
Nor the deep sad shadow in the lips of a lover
That is the challenge.
These are acclaimed;
They had to be written;
They were done well.

It is the timeful after,
After wanting is granted,
And a quiet, with eyes lighting
Distinct darkness,
Persists,
When nothing <u>must</u> be written
But the print of a tapering kiss
On the sloping arms of a lover.
It is easy to deny
The language of unrhymed conflict,
When the flow from self to self
Needs no explication,
And not one outsider,
No paint nor page,
Is needed to evoke
One whole loved being for another.

It is this that is left unsaid:
All the conscious, wakeful,
Daytime love

Whose beauty cannot be read in wild colors.
One hand into another:
A moment as gentle as silk
And long as the thread of history.

Awarded the Emily Chamberlain Cook Prize in Poetry,
UC Berkeley, 1956

RELLA LOSSY
1934–1996

Rella Lossy was a former member of the Iowa Poetry Workshop, where she studied with Robert Lowell, Karl Shapiro, and Wallace Fowlie. She received a B.A. in English from the University of California Berkeley (Phi Beta Kappa) and an M.A. in Creative Writing from San Francisco State University.

Her poems have been published in such magazines as *Chicago Review, ETC.*, and *The Critical Quarterly*. A chapbook of her poetry, *Audible Dawn*, was published by Holmgangers Press.

A playwright as well as a poet, Ms. Lossy was a member of The Dramatists Guild, and Poets & Writers Inc. For the past eight years she was a Lecturer at Boalt Hall School of Law, UC Berkeley, in Civil Trial Practice. In addition she was a consultant to the legal profession, conducting seminars, giving lectures, and leading workshops on a variety of topics.

Rella Lossy died at home just one week after sending the final copy of this book to the publisher.

ARTISTS

SUE SOMMERS
Metronomes

Sue Sommers works as an artist and educator in the Chicago area and has exhibited her watercolors and wood/metal cut–outs widely in the Mid–West. She is also the author of *Teaching from the Inside Out*, a guide for teachers in creative arts.

Sue and Rella met at International House, UC Berkeley in 1954, and have maintained a deep friendship ever since.

JUNE FELTER
The Middle Ages

June Felter studied at the San Francisco Art Institute and the Oakland Art Institute, and has exhibited work in major galleries in the U. S., Europe, and Asia. She has taught at colleges, institutes, and universities all over Northern California in a career spanning several decades.

June and Rella met during Rella's "middle ages" and have admired each other's work ever since.

JOAN COBITZ
Early On

Joan Cobitz – artist, teacher, cook – is a Chicagoan who lives in Savannah. She bakes bread for the local health food store, periodically teaches print making, and enjoys life with some close friends and her mongrel companion, Mango.

Joan and Rella grew up across the street from each other on Winthrop Avenue in Chicago, and began collaborating on art and poetry when they were in their teens.

All profits from the sale of this book go to *Commonweal Cancer Help Program.* For further information about Commonweal, write:

Commonweal
P.O. Box 316 • Bolinas, CA 94924
1–415–868–0970